Simon's Sensors: The Secret of the iPads

AUDITING MN, Volume 2

Erik van Mechelen

Published by Erik van Mechelen, 2025.

SIMON'S SENSORS: THE SECRET OF THE IPADS

First edition. April 30, 2025.

Copyright © 2025 Erik van Mechelen.

ISBN: 979-8230973737

Written by Erik van Mechelen.

Also by Erik van Mechelen

AUDITING MN

Auditing Minnesota: The 2022 SOS Campaign
Simon's Sensors: The Secret of the iPads

Standalone

Selections in Minnesota: Consequences of the 2020 Election and How
to Reclaim Control of Our Government

Watch for more at https://projectminnesota.com.

Table of Contents

#

INTRODUCTION - Discovering a Quiet Ritual

#

Throughout early 2025, there was a kind of religious dedication to electronic poll pads, especially those from a shell company called KNOWiNK—named the fastest growing private business in St. Louis Business Journal in 2021—itself sprouted out of thin air by Scott Leiendecker. One could reasonably ask, Was it even his software?

In Minnesota, there was an almost ritualistic use on each voting day in most of the counties and a new wave of rollouts had begun in 2022 (Hennepin County) to replace previous purchases and go for maximum coverage across as many of Minnesota's 87 counties as possible. I personally caught up with the story at the end of 2024, when the Anoka County Elections Integrity Team (ACEIT) had supported Mayor Weston Rolf (City of Oak Grove) to, along with his city council, cancel the leasing agreement with Anoka County.

This led to a felony threat in a letter from the Anoka County Elections Department in an unsigned letter that seemed to be contributed by the Anoka County Attorney Brad Johnson and which directly quoted Secretary of State Steve Simon.

The excitement, it seemed, was from a very small group. Even with the cost and their need to be replaced quite frequently, why did they want these electronic poll pads so badly? It wasn't exactly clear then—though there were hunches. What made people like me question more was the official suggestion to any election judges (election workers, in Minnesota) in Anoka County that if they decided to use paper poll books in the 2024 genera election, that the Anoka County Attorney would have no choice but to hand them felonies. This threat came only days before the 2024 election.

Meanwhile, few outside that circle, even those who had been skeptical about recently reported results from the overall computerized systems, realized the extent of the spread of this particular 'roster' technology, nor its likely decisive impact. When questioned, the narrative from those encouraging the march of the iPads was dogmatic, something like, These electronic devices are *just* a way to check-in and register voters, in a tone that invited more questions. And so it seemed there was much more to learn about these internet-capable tablets and everything they might enable. With so much noise and a few tangible efforts in the domain of elections in that year and the immediately preceding few, it is understandable that not so many Minnesotans were yet to notice the deeper motivations and thoughts—perhaps even a design—which led to their purchase and routine use.

Now, however, with the short list of changes needed to decentralize elections, to put them back in the hands of the people, to make them obviously transparent and understandable to all—perhaps only removing the electronic poll pads and using paper poll books (as was done for decades prior), is something with the power and authority of local governments, including cities, towns, and counties right here, right Now, in Minnesota.

At a time in the first half of the year 2025 when many are asking, What can be done?, the answer might simply be to not buy the iPads in the first place, or to cancel the existing contracts, and use paper, which is secure, auditable, and reliable, and therefore worthy of public trust.

On April 24, 2025 I learned that already 71 counties had deployed over 7,000 KNOWiNK electronic poll pads, which are in the case of the latest rollout iPads with cellular-internet capability and software enabling syncing inside a precinct and outside, to state-level databases such as the statewide voter registration system. The proof of the planning for such detailed data connections is in the official reports from The Minnesota Office of the Secretary of State's Electronic Task Force

Findings and Recommendations delivered January 31st, 2014, after a pilot in five (5) cities in three (3) counties in 2013, prior to the first major rollot in Hennepin County in 2016, and to many other counties in 2018. This task force included the Minnetonka City Clerk, David Maeda, who was the first clerk to use electronic poll pads already in 2009, and became the State Elections Director in 2019, appointed by Secretary of State, Steve Simon.

Though my research had begun perhaps a year or two earlier into the KNOWiNK poll pads, about the scale of the rollout in particular I learned from a presentation given by the Isanti County Auditor Angie Larson to the Isanti Township Officers on April 24, 2025. This presentation, as noted by Derek Lind of Ramsey (Anoka County), contained similar talking points to Anoka Elections Manager Tom Hunt's presentation on same from January 29, 2025, when Anoka County, having only purchased the iPads for its 128 precincts in 2018, was deciding whether to buy another round. On that evening, I was able to respond in about nine (9) minutes to a joint presentation that lasted about thirty (30) minutes from not only the Isanti County Auditor but also the Chisago County Auditor, Bridgette Konrad, along with choreographed questions from staff and friendlies in the audience—one from Cambridge said he might have a heart attack if the electronic devices were removed—to emphasize their various arguments about speed, convenience, and voter experience. (See https://projectminnesota.com/documents for the audio from that presenation as well as my nine-minute response, focusing on trust, cost, and impact—the transcript of my response also comes later in this book.)

This late April meeting came about two months after an Anoka County Government Operations Committee of the Whole decision on whether to approve the purchase of iPad Cellular Poll Pads in the amount of $271,437.50 and approving the extension amendment to Anoka County Contract #C0006472 with KNOWiNK, LLC from Feb 25, 2025 to Feb 24, 2025, with automatic renewals each year. The vote was 4-2 in favor with one (1) commissioner skipping the vote (not present). Two commissioners, John Heinrich, and Jeff Reinert, spoke against, and voted No, with Commissioner Heinrich raising a concern about the possibility of scalable fraud were it to occur (versus paper poll books), and Commissioner Reinert speaking to the brief history of the rollout and his opinion that the cities should get to choose (which happens to be in line with the current election statutes).

The dollar amount on the KNOWiNK contract is noted to emphasize the cost, however it is important to realize that these are being subsudized by the state either by grants or by suggesting more recently to use the VOTER Account allocations for this purpose. This way, the cost doesn't appear as high to the county without also noting that the counties can use such funds for *any* election administration activity, such as hiring election judges or temporary staff.

Calling around the state in April 2025, I further learned that Cass County had recently purchased replacement iPads as well, in early 2025. On the phone, the County Administrator was very happy with them. As are many of the staff. Interestingly, many of this small group that is in favor of them repeats similar talking points, almost as if these talking points come from a single source.

Having been previously excluded from a Benton County township meeting despite the invite from one of the county commissioners to speak about hand counting—admittedly a dangerous topic these days—it was clear in the Isanti Township Officer meeting how incisive the problem of information assymetry had become. In essence, with various staff and in this case not one but two county auditors (Isanti's and Chisago's) given access to these local decision makers, while preventing 'the other side' from having any air time, the I think detailed direction from the Minnesota Office of the Secretary of State would be messaged without any counter argument. (The full audio recordings of that evening are provided in at https://projectminnesota.com/documents.)

If reading in the first half of 2025, what do I want people to know?

1. These electronic poll pads probably allow precision cheating at the precinct level. Quoting others, mathmetician Draza Smith has said elections are a precinct level game. Such cheating at scale is becoming better understood through peer-reviewed work of the likes of Andrew Paquette (the Shift Cypher, the Spiral Algorithm) and by considering #3 below.

2. Meaningfully accessing 3rd-party vendor data is difficult as it typically is not subject to FOIA or data requests like government data is. However, by simply using paper poll books, those working at the precincts (and the voters) at least know their data isn't leaving the precinct throughout election day through an electronic device (at least not through the iPads... the electronic tabulators generally have modems installed which can connect to the internet).

3. But, at worst, it is possible that the coordinated electronic poll pad rollout (and its seeming coelescing behind a single company, KNOWiNK) suggests that it indeed might represent at minimum a local precinct level sensor in a larger PID controller scheme, if Patrick

Colbeck's findings of NIH-issued grant to develop a system to dynamically audit elections using electronic registration and voting systems (see US Patent 7549049 and Patrick Colbeck's findings in 2021[1]) are accurate: the abstract of the patent reads, in part: "In particular, the present invention provides false voting data associated with false voters to the voting systems..."

4. While Colbeck originally posted the Patent in 2021, his April 30, 2025 explanatory post[2] with hat tip from Sydney Powell who originally alerted him to it, led me to comment, "how much do you guys see KNOWiNK and similar being connected to this in real-time Now?", which Colbeck and Powell liked—South Dakota Canvassing Group, which did a deep dive update on BPro/KNOWiNK[3] responded, "exactly".

5a. Minnesota towns, cities, and counties should know or be reminded that these electronic poll pads are NOT mandatory. Staff, including attorneys, including the Secretary of State (as shown in quoted material in a 2024 Anoka County Elections Department letter) have argued and will probably continuing arguing that they can be made de facto or effectively mandatory if the head election official says so, which they argue is the county auditor. These arguments have major flaws and are refuted by a 118-page document linked to on projectminnesota.com/documents[4] as well as aceit.vote[5]. After sharing this document with at least one commissioner, Anoka County has not gone ahead with a vote on city autonomy as, according to Commissioner Jeff Reinert on February 2025, speaking in favor of city freedom and autonomy, said

---

1. https://letsfixstuff.org/2021/09/election-control-system-did-2020-election-get-an-eco-boost/

2. https://x.com/pjcolbeck/status/1917634115714834610https://x.com/pjcolbeck/status/1917634115714834610

3. https://southdakotacanvassinggroup.substack.com/p/where-did-bproknowink-go

4. http://projectminnesota.com/documents

5. http://aceit.vote

he had been promised—perhaps it is because the cities already have the choice.

5b. Even while the general meeting minutes found in Recommendations and Findings from the Electronic Roster Task Force from the Office of the Secretary of State show that the discussion of whether to mandate or not happened, the statutes themselves, which are the final word, suggest choice. If it is worse than that, if the statutes have been made to appear as though there is choice, when there isn't, then Minnesota voters should be on even higher alert. More likely, the choice to not mandate was made to allow the poll pads to be rolled out quietly and in waves to account for the lack of cell phone towers in certain areas within certain counties in Minnesota around 2016 to 2018.

#

Maybe some skeptical readers will question whether electronic poll pads enable cheating. That depends on how deeply one has thought about the overall electronic system, the legal gaps, and the piecemeal audits. But maybe those same readers will also agree that at minimum, paper rosters do not have internet capability and therefore cannot be viewed or updated remotely nor by a centralized source. Indeed, the suspicion that perhaps even the Minnesota Attorney General Keith Ellison, had somehow received access or been given information about real-time in-person in-precinct voting was raised by a tweet on his account, 3:57pm on November 3rd, 2020, which said in part that, "We don't have all of the votes we need quite yet."

#

If you've voted, great! Can you please call a friend? Spend a little time getting friends, fams, and folks out to the polls. We don't have all of the votes we need quite yet. So, help a friend (even a brand new friend) vote. Right now would be awesome.

3:57 PM · Nov 3, 2020 · Twitter for iPhone

188 Retweets   **876** Quote Tweets   **952** Likes

#

But as I've also learned from people like Walter Daugherity, in a brief discussiona about cast vote records in 2024, when one reveals that he has learned something about the system, the system is likely to adjust and not do exactly the same thing the next time. As former systems tester for the very labs that certify the election equipment, Clay Parikh has said in a Georgia hearing that there are thousands of ways to skin the cat.

This short book's purpose is to introduce readers and voters to what I learned and how I learned about the electronic poll pads—which as of today I want to start describing as sensors for the PID control scheme—by sharing a brief history of their rollout and then proceed into a snapshot of the current discussions at a number of counties, who are on the tail end of Minnesota's statewide rollout as I write this in April and May of 2025.

Will any counties, cities, or towns, say No? Read on and discover that some already have, the state's response to which made me realize we might really be onto something important which they didn't want us to know about...

#

CHAPTER 1 - Mayor Rick Weible Says, No Thank You

#

Even after deciding to research the overall election system, start to finish, including as many inputs, outputs, and influences I could find, the electronic poll pads initially eluded my attention. (The original version of *[S]elections in Minnesota* mentioned them only a little, though the third version, released in March 2025, now highlights them.) I cared about the electronic tabulators most, at first, and then about mail-in ballots (reminders came from people like Joe Oltmann) and the lax absentee ballot boards (the people who process the absentee ballots in each county, mostly unsupervised, which Susan Shogren Smith emphasized), and only after getting a handle on all this, friends started talking to me about these electronic poll pads, which it now seems obvious allow for precision cheating given they give a central view of precinct-level voting data. Sometime in 2024, I asked Erin Clements if we were right to focus on them in Minnesota, and she reminded me of the article she'd done with Jessica Pollema in 2023[1], and that she was convinced the cheating had migrated into these systems.

The first time I checked in on an electronic poll pad, which is just an iPad, internet-connected, with embedded software from KNOWiNK, a company I'd never heard of, I didn't think much of it. Afterall, it's just checking me in, right? They grab my digital signature—how or where this is stored or for what use I don't know, though conceivably this signature could be printed on, for example, an absentee ballot. Next, the poll pad through bluetooth sends a command to the small receipt printers and I bring to the ballots judge (election workers are called judges in MN even though they don't judge anything) who give me a

---

1. https://joehoft.com/shocking-exclusive-bpro-knowinks-uncertified-internet-connected-cloud-based-election-systems-are-foreign-influenced-and-used-to-illegally-process-election-results/

paper ballot, and after filling in a few ovals for politicians controlled by the parties, will bring that piece of paper to be fed into the electronic tabulator.

But what if, through the data syncs happening at that time through wifi hotspot (prior to 2024/2025) and then internet connection (and more recently through cellular internet connection), it was already known by someone monitoring the poll pads statewide, that I had voted? What if, further, that data was merged with L2 data to understand how I likely voted? Or combined with L2 *and* data pulled remotely from the electronic tabulators, which in Minnesota have modems enabled?

I should have asked more questions earlier on. Already in October of 2021, when I finally met Rick Weible, he mentioned during his presentation (if I recall) that he hacked into one of the electronic poll pads during the product demo to the city where he was mayor, St. Bonifacius, a municipality in Hennepin County.

In 2025, I learned from Rick that in addition to having breached the security of the iPad during the demo, Rick decided that the Disclaimer in the proposed agreement was the biggest reason for the 2016 rejection. There were no guarantees at all for the data to be accurate, complete and current, or even free from harmful code. He asked the city, So if we need an agreement, then they need our approval, don't they? Otherwise the county wouldn't need to send an agreement written to escape liability. Rick decided he would not be signing it because he didn't want to accept responsibility for low standards.

This letter, prepared for cities in Anoka County in January of 2025, goes into detail about 2016.

#

Date: 1/22/2025
RE: Cities Considering Poll Books

Dear City Council Members,

I am a former Mayor from the City of St. Bonifacius, MN, serving from 2006-2016 as the mayor. And during 2016, Hennepin County was the pilot county to test the Knowlnk Poll Books. During this testing phase, I was able to circumvent the security of the poll pads and had discussions with my Council and Hennepin County during that time. Our Council asked a lot more questions at that time about the county contracts and the support they were going to have with Knowlnk. After reviewing the materials our Council voted to not use the poll pads in 2016. The biggest concern was to ensure that the data would be accurate and the machines reliable. As a computer expert, and owning my own consulting company, there was no way I could sign a contract with the following language in it:

4.   DISCLAIMER, LIABILITY AND LIMITATION OF LIABILITY

COUNTY, BY AND THROUGH ITS DULY AUTHORIZED VENDOR, IS PROVIDING THE ELECTION EQUIPMENT ON AN AS-IS BASIS WITH NO SUPPORT WHATSOEVER. THERE IS NO WARRANTY OF MERCHANTABILITY, NO WARRANTY OF FITNESS FOR PARTICULAR USE, NO WARRANTY OF NON-INFRINGEMENT, NO WARRANTY REGARDING THE USE OF

THE INFORMATION OR THE RESULTS THEREOF AND NO OTHER WARRANTY OF ANY KIND, EXPRESS OR IMPLIED.

CITY ACKNOWLEDGES AND AGREES THAT COUNTY DOES NOT OWN OR CONTROL THE DATA SOURCE/SYSTEM NECESSARY FOR OPERATION OF THE ELECTION EQUIPMENT. WITHOUT LIMITING THE FOREGOING, COUNTY DOES NOT WARRANT THE PERFORMANCE OF THE ELECTION EQUIPMENT OR RELATED COMMUNICATIONS OR CONNECTIONS TO ANY DATA SOURCE/SYSTEM, THAT THE DATA SOURCE/SYSTEM WILL BE UNINTERRUPTED OR ERROR FREE, THAT THE DATA IS ACCURATE, COMPLETE AND CURRENT OR THAT DATA DEFECTS WILL BE CORRECTED, OR THAT THE DATA SOURCE/SYSTEM IS FREE OF HARMFUL CODE.

IN NO EVENT SHALL COUNTY BE LIABLE FOR ACTUAL, DIRECT, INDIRECT, SPECIAL, INCIDENTAL, CONSEQUENTIAL DAMAGES OR LOSS OF PROFIT, LOSS OF BUSINESS OR ANY OTHER FINANCIAL LOSS OR ANY OTHER DAMAGES EVEN IF COUNTY HAS BEEN ADVISED OF THE POSSIBILITY OF SUCH DAMAGE. COUNTY'S SOLE LIABILITY AND CITY'S SOLE AND EXCLUSIVE REMEDY FOR ANY DAMAGES RELATED TO THIS AGREEMENT, INCLUDING BUT NOT LIMITED TO LIABILITY FOR ELECTION EQUIPMENT NONPERFORMANCE, ERRORS OR OMISSIONS, SHALL BE LIMITED TO RESTORING OR CORRECTING THE ELECTION EQUIPMENT TO THE EXTENT AND DEGREE COUNTY IS CAPABLE OF PERFORMING THE SAME AND AS IS REASONABLY POSSIBLE UNDER THE PERTINENT CIRCUMSTANCES.

Please protect our elections by ensuring that the systems are protected, secure, and reliable. If there are no service guarantees, explicit protections or stated performance benchmarks, do not sign this type of contract. Do not hand over your elections to a third-party vendor, where you have no oversight, accountability or reliability. You should know what you are signing up for, remember paper poll books cannot be hacked remotely since they for sure can not connected to a Wi-Fi, internet or any network.

Rick Weible, Former Mayor – City of St. Bonifacius, MN
Election Cyber & Integrity Professional, Election Investigator,
Co-Author of the Gold Standard Elections – USCASE.ORG

#

Notice the paragraph again: CITY ACKNOWLEDGES AND AGREES THAT COUNTY DOES NOT OWN OR CONTROL THE DATA SOURCE/SYSTEM NECESSARY FOR OPERATION OF THE ELECTION EQUIPMENT. WITHOUT LIMITING THE FOREGOING, COUNTY DOES NOT WARRANT THE PERFORMANCE OF THE ELECTION EQUIPMENT OR RELATED COMMUNICATIONS OR CONNECIONTS TO

ANY DATA SOURCE/SYSTEM, THAT THE DATA SOURCE/ SYSTEM WILL BE UNINTERRUPTED OR ERROR FREE, THAT THE DATA IS ACCURATE, COMPLETE AND CURRENT OR THAT DATA DEFECTS WILL BE CORRECTED, OR THAT THE DATA SOURCE/SYSTEM IS FREE OF HARMFUL CODE.

Can anyone truly fault a mayor and his council for voting No in light of this contract? The fact that there's no guarantee "the data source/ system is free of harmful code" is particularly glaring.

After Mayor Rick Weible told them that he hacked the electronic device, Hennepin County sent the second letter which is produced here, speaking about how secure things are, which calls into question the need for such language in the agreement.

#

Hennepin County Resident and Real Estate Services

A-600 Hennepin County Government Center
Minneapolis, Minnesota 55487-0060

June 27, 2016
The Honorable Rick Weible, Mayor of St. Bonifacius
Re: License agreement for use of Hennepin County electronic poll books

Dear Mayor Weible:

This letter is to confirm that in the proposed agreement between Hennepin County and the City of St. Bonifacius for the city's use of electronic poll books purchased by Hennepin County, the source of the data that Hennepin County will use to populate the devices is the Statewide Voter Registration System database, as maintained by the Office of the Secretary of State and that the electronic poll book system meets all legally required security standards.

Hennepin County is required by Minnesota Statutes §201.225 to certify to the Office of the Secretary of State that the electronic poll book system meets the requirements in the law, including security, reliability, and networking standards established by the Office of the Secretary of State in consultation with MN.IT. After acceptance testing and architecture review, the county has made that certification to the state. (The same section also grants the county the authority to designate precincts to use electronic poll books.) In addition to those standards, the system has also been approved by Hennepin County's Architecture Review Board and the system has undergone a threat assessment conducted by Hennepin County IT Security Operations, and the resulting risk mitigation plan has been implemented.

As you know, the successful deployment of these devices in Hennepin County supports a number of strategic elections goals, including reducing wait times at the polls by decreasing the amount of time election judges spend checking in each voter, increasing the accuracy of voter check-in data, and enabling Hennepin County to perform mail absentee ballot tasks that in the past the city would have had to perform. We welcome feedback from the city on ways to improve the electronic poll book system and will make every effort with our vendor to make sure this solution works well for St. Bonifacius.

Sincerely,

Ginny Gelms, Elections Manager
Hennepin County Resident and Real Estate Services

#

Not only do they speak about how great the electronic devices are or will be, they express interest in more feedback on how to improve the electronic poll book system. Was this Hennepin County's way of confirming the hack that Rick Weible found while hiding what he did? Why else ask for feedback?

I was also able to also receive a copy of this memo through the Hennepin County data request portal, although my request was more detailed:

#

All email communication between Hennepin County officials and staff and the City of St. Bonifacius officials and staff, including but not limited to Jim Howitt (jim.howitt@hennepin.us), Ginny Gelms, Kristin Sepeta, and Brenda Fisk (brendafisk@st-bonifacius.mn.us) and Rick Weible (then Mayor of St. Bonifacius) regarding:

- electronic roster KNOWiNK usage agreement for city in 2016
- electronic roster KNOWiNK county purchase agreement in 2016
- discussions about whether KNOWiNK poll pads were required for St. Bonifacius

- any emails referencing in any way the KNOWiNK poll pads or electronic rosters or related statutes, such as Minn Stat §201.225 This may be a large PDF document once rolled up, so thank you in advance for preparing the digital file. Erik

Status : Full Release w/o Redactions

#

To be clear, this status of "full release w/o redactions" is false given that I only received the one memo as the emails from that era in 2016 had apparently been deleted. It seems that memos are kept longer than emails.

The good news for Minnesota history is that Rick Weible kept a number of these emails. For example...

#

Brenda Fisk

From:	Jim Howitt <Jim.Howitt@hennepin.us>
Sent:	Wednesday, April 27, 2016 9:22 AM
To:	BrendaFisk@St-Bonifacius.mn.us
Cc:	Ginny Gelms; Kristin Sepeta
Subject:	RE: e poll book agreement

Hi Brenda,

Yes, use of the poll books is required. We will not be providing paper rosters for manual sign ins. The electronic poll books are an important part of increasing the efficiency and accuracy of the voter check in and election day registration process. In addition, the poll books are an necessary part of getting absentee ballots counted, and therefore results released, in a timely way on election night.

If there are specific concerns you or your council have please contact Ginny and she will be happy to address them.

Our staff is out of the office the rest of the week, so are not available by phone, but Ginny and I are both monitoring email.

Thank you,

Jim Howitt | Administrative Assistant | Hennepin County Elections
300 S 6th St | Minneapolis MN 55487-0012
612-348-0306 | Fax 612-348-2151
||Jim.Howitt@hennepin.us | ·· www.hennepin.us/elections

-----Original Message-----
From: BrendaFisk@St-Bonifacius.mn.us
Sent: Tuesday, April 26, 2016 4:08 PM
To: Jim Howitt <Jim.Howitt@hennepin.us>
Subject: RE: e poll book agreement

Hi Jim, Are we required to use this equipment. The st. boni council would like to continue using the manual sign in roster. Brenda -----Original Message-----
From: Jim Howitt [mailto:Jim.Howitt@hennepin.us]
Sent: Tuesday, April 05, 2016 9:00 AM
To: fisk@visi.com
Subject: e poll book agreement

Hello,

Attached is a user agreement between your city and Hennepin County for the electronic poll books and the related hardware. This agreement specifies the number of units your city is receiving and the duties of both the county and city. As we've mentioned previously, there is no cost to the cities for the poll books. Cities receiving more than 10 poll pads will notice that Meraki wireless access points are included in their agreements. Meraki units are for the purpose of allowing many poll pads to download data simultaneously without network congestion. We are currently working with Knowink on the installation details and will have more information for you soon.

#

It can be seen in this email thread that Brenda from St. Bonifacius has asked if St. Bonifacius is being required to use the equipment, and Jim Howitt from Hennepin County responds in the affirmative. Readers should make a note of this as already in 2016 the narrative was that they are required. Why then was there no penalty when St. Bonifacius said, No Thank You?

Note also that the Administrateive Assistant within the Hennepin County Elections department also says "We will not be providing paper rosters for manual sign ins." If Hennepin County had chosen not to provide these, it would have been a violation of the election codes as well because paper backups are required at every precinct. So to state such in an email in an apparent attempt to persuade St. Bonifacius is quite remarkable. Why not simply give accurate information, which is that indeed it was the option for St. Bonifacius as the municipality to decide? Let the history show what was attempted and how subtle the techniques of persuasion were.

In 2016, St. Bonifacius was the lone municipality to decline the electronic poll pad contract with Hennepin County, which had the contract with KNOWiNK, and the city continued using its paper poll books, which, as one would expect, worked just fine.

#

#

CHAPTER 2 - The 2013 Electronic Roster Task Force

#

In early 2025 a friend sent me the 75-page report from the Electronic Task Force: Findings and Recommendations, from the Office of the Secretary of State, published on January 31, 2014. This was one of those moments that gets ones attention, a kind of sign to look into it a bit more. A few months later, I took about a week to produce the book you're now holding. But reading that report in full led me to a few new questions and reminded me that this electronic poll pad rollout has been carefully orchestrated. The arrangement probably goes well beyond Minnesota—KNOWiNK is in about 30 states and is now cheerfully certified by the Election Assistance Commission. This short book will focus on Minnesota's rollout.

As the task force report notes, David Maeda's Minnetonka first used electronic poll pads in 2009, and KNOWiNK itself was founded in 2011, but perhaps the official beginning of the electronic poll pad movement seems to have been in 2013, when the Minnesota Legislature authorized the Electronic Roster Task Force.

From the document—produced in full on projectminnesota.com/documents[1], we learn that the Electronic Roster Task Force consists of the following 15 members. I wonder how many of the following are still proud of their contributions... they either didn't understand the magnitude of the changes they were bring in, or they did:

- The director of the Department of Public Safety, Division of Vehicle Services, or
  designee: **Pat McCormack;**
- The secretary of state, or designee: **Secretary of State Mark**

---

1.   http://projectminnesota.com/documents

"

Ritchie;

- An individual designated by the secretary of state, from the elections division in the Office of the Secretary of State: Elections Director **Gary Poser;**
- The chief information officer of the state of Minnesota, or designee; **Commissioner Carolyn Parnell;**
- One county auditor appointed by the Minnesota Association of County Officers: **Debby Erickson**, Crow Wing County;
- One town election official appointed by the Minnesota Association of Townships: **Barb Welty**, Kathio Township;
- One city election official appointed by the League of Minnesota Cities: **David Maeda**, City of Minnetonka;
- One school district election official appointed by the Minnesota School Boards Association: **Grace Wachlarowicz;**
- One representative appointed by the speaker of the house of representatives: **Rep. Carolyn Laine** (DFL – Columbia Heights);
- One representative appointed by the minority leader of the house of representatives: **Rep. Tim O'Driscoll** (R - Sartell);
- One senator appointed by the senate Subcommittee on Committees of the Committee on Rules and Administration: **Sen. Terri Bonoff** (DFL – Minnetonka);
- One senator appointed by the senate minority leader: **Sen. Mary Kiffmeyer** (R- Big Lake);
- One person appointed by the governor, familiar with electronic roster technology but who does not represent a specific vendor of the technology: **Max Hailperin;** and
- Two election judges appointed by the governor: **Vaughn Bodelson** and **Kathy Bonnifield**.

#

One name missing from this task force seems to be then District 46B Represenative Steve Simon, who served in the Minnesota House since 2004, and in 2013 and 2014 chaired the House Elections Committee, contributing to legislation for online voter registration, no-excuse absentee voting, easier voting access for oversees voters, and actively opposed Voter ID.

Given his involvement in these sweeping changes, it is unlikely that he was not connected to the electronic task force. Indeed, would it be suprising if he were not the chief author of HF1420 which initialized the task force? He was.

Note too, that Max Hailperin, the single governor-appointee to the task force, to this day writes articles in outlets like MinnPost in favor of many of now Secretary Simon's contributions. It would not be a shock if at some point it is discovered that Mr. Hailperin collaborated on past legislation and current, even in 2025, since it is obvious that most legislators do not actively contribute to the bills they chief author, co-author, or sponsor. Secretary Simon may be an exception to that.

Then and now, it seems that the Secretary is focused on increasing voter registrations, voter turnout, and the number of absentee/mail-in voters. A simple review of the Governor's annual budgets from recent years and the proposed FY2026/2027 Revised Budget Recommendations for the Secretary of State[2] show not only the enormous amounts of money available to achieve these goals (FY2022 = \$18M, FY2023 = \$15, FY2024 = \$27M, FY2025(estimate) = \$26M, FY2026(proposed) = \$23M, FY2027(proposed) = \$23M) but also that the Office of the Secretary of State is measured on these accessibility metrics but not on whether the system can be easily auditable, nor in how well it, in conjunction with the Attorney General's Office, enforces election codes.

---

2.   https://mn.gov/mmb-stat/documents/budget/2026-27-biennial-budget-books/governors-revised-march/secretary-of-state.pdf

#

RESULTS

The Office measures its performance by the indicators set out in the table below. Each of these measures indicates the Office's strategies are working.

Type of Measure	Name of Measure	Previous	Current	Dates
Quantity	Number of registered voters	3,392,082	3,594,940	2020/2024
Result	Voter Turnout	2,968,281 (74.72%)	3,292,997 (79.96%)	11/8/2016 11/3/2020
Quantity	General Absentee and Mail Ballots Returned by Election Day	638,846	672,571	11/6/2018 11/8/2022
Result	General Absentee Ballots Acceptance Rate	98.57%	98.37%	11/6/2018 11/8/2022
Quantity	Number of applicants and participants served by Safe at Home in calendar year	4,589	5,286	2021/2023
Quantity	Cost of postage to forward mail to Safe at Home participants	$102,575	$113,034	2021/2023
Quantity	Number of victim advocates who voluntarily partner with Safe at Home	311	340	2021/2023
Quantity	Number of active households as of last day of calendar year	1,745	1,947	2021/2023
Quantity	Number of new business filings	93,184	97,706	2021/2023
Quantity	Number of business web filings	502,571	536,004	2021/2023
Quantity	Number of business mail and counter filings	24,145	26,014	2021/2023
Quantity	Number of UCC/Tax Lien & CNS web filings	113,491	104,444	2021/2023
Quantity	Number of open appointment applications	3,269	3,431	2021/2023
Quantity	Official Documents filed	3,791	5,415	2021/2023

#

While there is much of potential interest to historians to understand how the origins of these poll pads came together, this chapter will focus simply on a few points related to data flows, internet connectivity to achieve that, and whether the electronic poll pads would be mandated to push out paper.

On Page 10 of the PDF version, which is page 7 of the Electronic Roster Task Force: Findings & Recommendations—found in full at https://projectminnesota.com/documents, David Maeda is documenting benefits of using the electronic devices for election day registration.

#

- Once SVRS is programmed for the 2013 pilot project, will allow for electronic data to be directly uploaded into statewide voter registration system
#

Then, on page 8 and 9...

C. Data Security in Electronic Rosters and the Ability to Connect Rosters Throughout the State

The task force was required to research "data security in electronic rosters [and] the statewide voter registration system" and "the ability of precincts across the state to connect an electronic roster to a secure network to access the statewide voter registration system." 2013 Minn. Laws, Ch. 131, Art. 4, Sec. 2, Subd. 3(4) and (6).

The task force researched this issue by hearing presentations from the Office of Secretary of State's Elections Director Gary Poser and IT staff Matt McCollough. The presentation covered the data contained in the Statewide Voter Registration System, the data provided to election judges in paper rosters, the current security in place regarding the Statewide Voter Registration System, and the security and technological challenges of allowing all polling locations to have access to the Statewide Voter Registration System on election day. Other task force members also discussed internet connectivity issues both in urban and greater Minnesota polling locations.

Note the language, "the security and technological challenges of allowing all polling locations to have access to the Statewide Voter Registration System on election day". This part of the document gives insight into the more powerful capability nested within the architecture of the overall electronic voting system. Already in 2013, during the pilot program, those involved were discussing exactly how to technically accomplish precinct connectivity to the state's source of truth for election data, the Statewide Voter Registration System.

In Anoka County Election Manager Tom Hunt's presentation on January 29, 2025, he said that, Hypothetically, *he* could see the number of ballots that had been voted (and remaining) at every precinct in the county. If the Elections Manager has access, who else does? The County Auditor? What about adminstrators at the State level? What about administrators at KNOWiNK? It can be asked again for emphasis... What exactly are these devices capable of?

#

Also discussed in the Findings and Recommendations were very general minutes detailing whether the electronic poll pads should be made mandatory or not.

The paragraph of interest is from the December 9, 2013 meeting: "Members then discussed the following items: whether to authorize an additional pilot, whether the use of ePollbooks should be voluntary or mandatory, whether there should be a paper back-up for pre- registered voters, whether there should be a paper VRA for same day registrants, whether to build or buy ePollbook software, data security requirements, whether photos should be included in ePollbooks, the timeline for the implementation of any task force recommendations, and the costs associated with ePollbooks. "

The statutes eventually were the final result—even this task force wrote draft legislation—which did *not* mandate them. In fact, paper poll books would remain to be used in 2016 and even during the larger rollout in 2018, in part perhaps because cell phone towers weren't available throughout all areas and counties of Minnesota. Or, perhaps, because it was best not to mandate something which was aimed to stay under the radar.

Now, having examined the findings from this task force as of early 2014, let's jump ten years to 2024...

#

CHAPTER 3 - The Oak Grove Way

#

I first went to Oak Grove for ACEIT's January 29, 2024 presentation. Since, The Oak Grove Way has been a method to describe ending use of electronic poll pads and instead using paper poll books, requesting more of their precincts and down ballot races to be audited in the normal post election review hand count, and to take back the processing of absentee ballots, which many municipalities have outsourced to their counties.

Readers may wonder why cities and towns would simply not order there ballots to be hand counted. That is because, after myself and others spoke about this in 2022, the Legislature in 2024 amended the statutes to say that election judges (election workers) must immediately seal ballots on election night once polls close.

What's relevant in this book is that Oak Grove went first. It was the first city to cancel its agreement with its county, in this case Anoka County, for the electronic poll pads. It did so before the 2024 general election and then again in 2025. The City of Ramsey (in Anoka County) also cancelled theirs after the 2024 election.

But Oak Grove doing so in 2024 seemed to trigger a response from both the Secretary of State and the Anoka County Elections Department, as we'll see in the next chapter.

Note for the moment the resolution that follows (from 2025).

RESOLUTION 2025-032

CITY OF OAK GROVE
COUNTY OF ANOKA
STATE OF MINNESOTA

USE OF ELECTRONIC POLL ROSTERS

NOW, THEREFORE, BE IT RESOLVED, by the City Council of the City of Oak Grove, Minnesota that:

1. City staff are directed to engage with Anoka County, the Minnesota Office of the Secretary of State, and any other governmental entity to provide for the discontinuation of electronic poll rosters at city precincts pursuant to Resolution 24-101.

2. Staff are hereby directed and authorized to negotiate and renegotiate any agreement between the City and Anoka County to discontinue the use of electronic poll rosters at city precincts.

3. Staff are hereby authorized to take all other actions reasonably necessary to accomplish the goals of this resolution, including, but not limited to providing notice pursuant to Minnesota Statutes, section 201.225.

Adopted by the City Council this 24th day of February 2025.

____
Weston Rolf, Mayor

ATTEST:

____
Britt Pease, Deputy City Clerk

(Seal)

#

To emphasize, this was actually the second resolution from Oak Grove, the first coming prior to the November 5, 2024 election. I credit ACEIT with preparing the city council there with a working understanding about the electronic poll pads dating back to a presentation the group made after an invite from Oak Grove on January 29, 2024, a presentation I attended in person. I note this here to remind readers that it is relationships that connect us as humans and the combination of representatives and ordinary people—doing extraodinary work, some say—to outmaneuver considerable censorship regimes, inter-office pressure, and MN OSS budgets surpassing $20 million per annum. While one man, Mayor Weston Rolf, is required to rally his city council, doing so often is not done without knowing support exists and will endure. The test of this kind of support shows itself again when we get to the Isanti Township Officer meeting a few chapters from now.

For the moment, let's see what the reaction was from Anoka County, with aid from the Secretary of State, to the news that Oak Grove had cancelled its electronic poll pad agreement, the first cancellation of its kind, keeping in mind that Mayor Rick Weible's St. Bonifacius city council had declined the contract entirely from Hennepin County back in 2016... this was the first overt counter over eight years later, and it struck at the soft underbelly of the precinct-level cheat system.

#

CHAPTER 4 - Felonies for Using Paper Poll Books?

\#

A strange letter went out just a few days before the November 5, 2024 general election to all Anoka County election judges (again, this is what we call election workers in Minnesota). With each passing day, it is perhaps a letter that those involved regret sending.

\#

Anoka County
PROPERTY RECORDS & TAXATION DIVISION
Elections & Voter Registration

TO: **HEAD ELECTION JUDGES FOR THE 2024 GENERAL ELECTION**

FROM: **ANOKA COUNTY ELECTIONS DEPARTMENT**

As you prepare for next week's election, the Anoka County Elections Department wishes to provide you with some additional information regarding the use of electronic pollbooks in Anoka County polling places. There has been some discussion this year in various cities about a desire to use paper rosters rather than the electronic pollbooks that Anoka County has used for many years. This memo will clarify the requirement that all precincts **must** use electronic pollbooks during the 2024 general election and give you information that you can use should anyone ask you to violate Minnesota election law.

Minnesota Statute Section 201.225 governs the use of electronic rosters, otherwise known as electronic pollbooks. The relevant portion of that statute states as follows:

> A county, municipality, or school district may use electronic rosters for any election. In a county, municipality, or school district that uses electronic rosters, the head elections official may designate that some or all of the precincts use electronic rosters.

Id. at Subd. 1.

Anoka County has committed to the use of electronic rosters for the 2024 election. The 2024 election is a statewide election, and therefore the head elections official for purposes of Section 201.225 is the head elections official of Anoka County. Anoka County has long designated its County Auditor as the county's head elections official.

In the official capacity as the head elections official, the Anoka County Auditor has determined that all precincts within Anoka County will use electronic pollbooks for the 2024 election. Pursuant to the ordinary process, the County Auditor notified the Secretary of State that Anoka County and all its precincts will use electronic rosters during the 2024 statewide election and that Anoka County's electronic rosters meet all the requirements imposed by Section 201.225. That final certification was due 30 days before the election, and Anoka County complied with that requirement. Now that the deadline for final certification has passed, the County Auditor does not have the ability or authority to change her mind in an effort to certify use of a different system, or to use different systems in different communities, for the 2024 election.

Minnesota law does not give local government units working with the county the right to choose procedures different from the one certified by the county's head elections official during a statewide election. No city, school district, township, or individual wards or precincts may adopt procedures different than the one certified to the Secretary of State by the head elections official. The Minnesota Secretary of State has provided the following guidance to Anoka County:

Under Minnesota law, the head election official for a county, municipality, or school district that uses electronic rosters may designate that some or all of the precincts may use electronic rosters. Minn. Stat. § 201.225, subd. 1. The head election official for state general elections is the county auditor. Minnesota law makes clear this official is in charge of administering state general elections at the local level. *See* Minn. Stat. § 201.018 (making the county auditor the chief registrar of voters); Minn. Stat. § 204B.27, subd. 5 (stating that county auditors are responsible for training local election officials and election judges); Minn. Stat. § 204D.11 (making the county auditor in charge of developing the state general election ballot).

The reference to the duties of head election officials for municipalities and school district under the electronic roster statute is simply to make clear that officials charged with administering municipal elections under Chapter 205 and school district elections under Chapter 205A have the same authority to determine whether electronic rosters are used in those elections when they are held on different dates from the state general election.

While I understand some have suggested that the principal election officials for counties, municipalities, and school districts each have the independent authority to determine the use of electronic rosters for their precincts, that is an unreasonable interpretation of Section 201.225. Such a result would suggest that county, municipal, and school district officials could issue contradictory orders to precincts in their respective jurisdictions, particularly when state, county, local, and school district races appear on the ballot together.

Section 201.225 makes clear that there is a single head election official for purposes of determining the use of electronic rosters. Because county auditors have supervisory authority over local officials for the state general election, they are considered the head election official for purposes of this statute.

The law is clear that individual or local official decisions not to follow the head election official's directions and interference with the election process will result in serious legal trouble for those involved. Refusing or declining to follow the head election official's direction to use electronic rosters and pollbooks in all Anoka County precincts would constitute a violation of numerous Minnesota election laws. For election judges, Minnesota Statute Section 204C.41 provides that any election judge who refuses to perform a required act is guilty of a felony. Under Minnesota Statute Section 201.27, any "officer, deputy, clerk, or other employee" who refuses to comply with the election laws is also guilty of a felony.

Minnesota law also imposes legal consequences on anyone who interferes with an election judge or other election official. Minnesota Statute §211B.076 makes it a gross misdemeanor to improperly influence an election official with regard to that official's performance of their duties. In 2023, the Minnesota Legislature enacted Section 211B.075, which also makes it a gross misdemeanor to interfere with the voting process through either intimidation or deceptive practices. Encouraging an election official to violate the procedures established by Anoka County's head elections official and certified to the Secretary of State would constitute a deceptive practice under Minnesota law.

Minnesota Statute Section 201.275 provides that "If there is probable cause for instituting a prosecution, the county attorney shall proceed according to the generally applicable standards regarding the prosecutorial functions and duties of a county attorney." This is a mandatory, non-discretionary duty. When there is probable cause of a violation and a good faith and reasonable belief that a criminal offense can be proved beyond reasonable doubt at the time of trial, the statute does not give the county attorney discretion to look the other way and ignore a violation of the election laws. If an investigation confirms that anyone has interfered with the use of electronic pollbooks in any Anoka County precinct during the 2024 election, the county attorney must prosecute the offender.

While the county attorney can consider the generally applicable standards regarding the prosecutorial functions and duties of a county attorney, he cannot simply turn a blind eye to actual or threatened violations – regardless of his personal beliefs. Moreover, the civil attorneys in the county attorney's office also have an ongoing duty and responsibility to represent Anoka County Elections and the County Auditor in their efforts to administer and oversee free and fair elections throughout the county.

Simply put, the overall legal advice that has been given to Anoka County Elections for the benefit and protection of local election officials and election judges for the 2024 election is to follow Minnesota law.

#

It is notable to make a connection back to 2016 at this point.

Note that this same assertion was being made already then to try to convince the mayor of St. Bonifacius to reconsider his council's decision to NOT use the electronic poll pads, but instead use paper rosters. Also, remember, they did *not* use them and there were no penalties or legal action taken against them for not doing so, despite the following documents expressing that St. Bonifacius must use them and that they would not be provided paper poll books.

The email is reproduced below again (as it was in a previous chapter) to emphasize the curious similarity of arguments from two separate counties about nine years apart.

#

Brenda Fisk

From:	Jim Howitt <Jim.Howitt@hennepin.us>
Sent:	Wednesday, April 27, 2016 9:22 AM
To:	BrendaFisk@St-Bonifacius.mn.us
Cc:	Ginny Gelms; Kristin Sepeta
Subject:	RE: e poll book agreement

Hi Brenda,

Yes, use of the poll books is required. We will not be providing paper rosters for manual sign ins. The electronic poll books are an important part of increasing the efficiency and accuracy of the voter check in and election day registration process. In addition, the poll books are an necessary part of getting absentee ballots counted, and therefore results released, in a timely way on election night.

If there are specific concerns you or your council have please contact Ginny and she will be happy to address them.

Our staff is out of the office the rest of the week, so are not available by phone, but Ginny and I are both monitoring email.

Thank you,

Jim Howitt | Administrative Assistant | Hennepin County Elections
300 S 6th St | Minneapolis MN 55487-0012
612-348-0306 | Fax 612-348-2151
||Jim.Howitt@hennepin.us | ·· www.hennepin.us/elections

-----Original Message-----
From: BrendaFisk@St-Bonifacius.mn.us
Sent: Tuesday, April 26, 2016 4:08 PM
To: Jim Howitt <Jim.Howitt@hennepin.us>
Subject: RE: e poll book agreement

Hi Jim, Are we required to use this equipment. The st. boni council would like to continue using the manual sign in roster. Brenda -----Original Message-----
From: Jim Howitt [mailto:Jim.Howitt@hennepin.us]
Sent: Tuesday, April 05, 2016 9:00 AM
To: fisk@visi.com
Subject: e poll book agreement

Hello,

Attached is a user agreement between your city and Hennepin County for the electronic poll books and the related hardware. This agreement specifies the number of units your city is receiving and the duties of both the county and city. As we've mentioned previously, there is no cost to the cities for the poll books. Cities receiving more than 10 poll pads will notice that Meraki wireless access points are included in their agreements. Meraki units are for the purpose of allowing many poll pads to download data simultaneously without network congestion. We are currently working with Knowink on the installation details and will have more information for you soon.

#

Bob, a member of ACEIT, has in early 2025 produced both a 31-page and then a 118-page document detailing a legal argument which, in short, says that municipalities decide, unless they give their decision-making authority to the county.

In other words, no matter what the county says, no matter what the auditors or election managers want to do, even if the county buys a huge number of electronic poll pads, and even if the Minnesota Secretary of State really, really wants the precinct-level sensors to be used, it is actually still up to the city or town to decide if they want to use them. Conversely, if the county said we have to use paper, a city or town could potentially go directly to KNOWiNK or some other vendor to get electronic devices for check-in and registration.

With this context, it seemed a bit premature for Anoka County to be voting to purchase a new batch of electronic poll pads in February 2025 when they hadn't asked all the cities whether they even wanted to continue with them. A point, which, we will see next, was actually made by one of the commissioners.

#

CHAPTER 5 - Two Commissioners Speak Against Electronic Poll Pads

\#

Several ACEIT members were in attendance at the February 2025 Anoka County Commissioner meeting, one sitting front row holding a poster of the Trojan Horse image featured in a previous article I'd written summarizing the dangers of poll pads, which have been slightly expanded upon so far in this book. Of course I give credit to Derek for the idea of the Trojan Horse, itself with its own nuances and relevant historically, but an apt metaphor to describe the quiet rollout of a system that I think has an outsized impact on producing sophisticated and precise election results in a difficult-to-detect manner.

\#

\#

This is a partial transcript from the important February 2025 Anoka County Commissioner meeting with only John Heinrich's and Jeff Reinert's key moments.

#

SCHULTE: The next item is #5, considering the purchase of iPad Cellular Poll Pads in the amount of $271,437.50 and approving the extension amendment to Anoka County Contract #C0006472 with KNOWiNK, LLC from Feb 25, 2025 to Feb 24, 2025, with automatic renewals each year.

#

HEINRICH: Thank you, Mr. Chair. I'm going to vote No on this today.

Nothing is 100 percent secure, but I do feel that paper poll pads are more secure than electronic poll pads.

If there is a nefarious actor trying to gain voter information through the poll pad system, that is certainly scalable. And that's my concern, the scalability of possible fraud.

There's less chance of fraud taking place, I feel, with paper poll pads versus the electronics.

Paper is not without some cost, and less efficiency maybe than the electronic pads. But for me that's a concern of mine, the scalability because of the use of electronics, where if fraud were to happen on paper, it would just be less scalable.

And for that reason I'm voting No today Mr. Chair.

#

REINERT: Yeah so, I'm not going to be supporting this as well, but for a lot of different reasons, really.

So we started using these poll pads in 2018. Up until 2018 we used paper rosters. They worked fine obviously. I think that there wouldn't be anybody that said they didn't otherwise you'd be saying every election prior to 2018 had a problem.

So they work. They're probably a little more cumbersome.

I've been trying to, I guess, have discussions at the county here for about a year, year and a half about just giving cities the autonomy to use the paper or use the poll pad.

Because the more that I try to bring forward that conversation, the more that I'm told that the poll pads really aren't that big a deal.

And it's true, the poll pad doesn't carry any votes, hold any votes, it's basically a roster.

You've got the paper roster, you've got the electronic roster that's on a poll pad. It's kind of a spreadsheet that's on a poll pad.

Well, if it's that low bar, what's the big deal?

To me, I don't really care if a city uses a paper roster or an electronic roster.

I just want to allow them the freedom, the autonomy, to do what they want.

I keep getting told that we're going to have a vote on this board about it, about that topic, about that question. And it might fail, it might succeed, but I've been trying to have it come before this board for a very long time.

I'm told now that we are going to have it at an upcoming committee meeting and then it would come before this board.

But for me it's all about procedure too. We should probably have that vote first, identify the cities that want these poll pads and not want these poll pads. And then, have some time pass to have cities answer that question, Yes or No, and then we would know which cities want them and which don't, and then you go buy the poll pads.

Yeah, for me it's about procedure, it's about autonomy, and I don't really care if you use poll pads or not. But it should be left up to the cities and the county shouldn't be lording over all the cities and saying, You will be doing it this way.

...

Just a final comment and I'm not going to jump on anyone up here I mean they all have their own opinions, and fine.

But I do think I want to correct one thing. I don't believe the board in 2018 did vote. I think it was administratively implemented change to have the cities use poll pads. And I believe only one city actually voted on the topic, strangely enough one of the cities that now don't want them.

But anyway, if they're as secure as everyone says, if they're as low bar as they are, that it's just a spreadsheet on an electronic device, I mean why do we care what cities use?

To me it's about freedom and autonomy. Drive a Chevy or a Ford truck, I mean, like you said, email, mail a letter, some people still like to mail letters. It's more to me about let cities do what they want to do. If there's truly no difference, let cities do what they want to do.

#

It was great to hear two commissioners in Heinrich speak about the scalability of potential fraud and Reinert on city autonomy, which is actually in line with the current Minnesota Statutes.

For emphasis it will now be repeated that even though Commissioner Reinert spoke (in the transcript above) about being assured the city autonomy question would come to a vote, that perhaps after reading or catching wind of the 118-page legal argument viewable on https://projectminnesota.com/documents, it was realized that such a vote would be moot.

Even though the vote went 4-2 in favor with one of the seven total commissioners absent, the political trend toward questioning the poll pads would not stop in Anoka. The county directly to the north, Isanti County, was being offered poll pads as well.

#

CHAPTER 6 - Isanti Township Officer Meeting

#

On the evening of April 24, 2025, at the Isanti County Government Center's commissioner board room, after the Isanti County Auditor Angie Larson, with support from Chisago County Auditor Bridgitte Konrad, and staff, presented for about 30 minutes, one of the Isanti commissioners said he wanted to hear from the other people here, refering to myself, Derek, and Joe. Val, the chair of the Isanti Township Officer meeting looked to me and I stood, approaching the table where Angie's computer was. She moved it out of the way even though I did not have a computer but instead glanced down at my notes I'd scribbled before the meeting with Derek and Joe, and added to during Angie's presentation. (Angie's full presentation audio can be found on https://projectminnesota.com/documents)

#

ERIK: Good evening, township officers. My name is Erik van Mechelen, and I'm here tonight with Derek and Joe right here, members of ACEIT, which is the Anoka County Election Integrity Team. So just south of you, and it's great to have just probably only three minutes to share a few points here, because I think there's been already some great questions about these, but just a bit of my background. I ran for SOS in 2022, I worked in IT at Target Corporation, and I've written two short books on this topic, consolidating the research over the last three years that I've done.

So this group, the ACEIT team, came together about three years ago. They meet every Monday. They're focused exclusively on election reform. So they're a very knowledgeable group.

Why are we here? I think this, I mean, it was first on the points that Alan made for tonight of his Commissioner group. It's also my number one issue that I think about and talk about. So I'm just going to make three points, because this group and the commissioner body, as well as the townships, has a really interesting and impactful choice they can make, where the legislature has taken away a lot of your choices. You still have this choice.

So the three points are around trust, cost, and then I'm going to really lay into that impact piece here. Here we are in 2025 we've been through a lot.

So with the trust. A few points under that. Historically, we've used paper. I hear the history of Cambridge, but historically we've used paper. It's secure, it's transparent, auditable, verifiable. It's difficult to cheat with paper.

The audit logs in the current system are not shared with this system in our current process. They could be not currently shared. That would probably be a legislative change.

Once again, on the trust, these electronic systems can be hacked. But actually, it's not a hypothetical. In 2016, the mayor of St. Bonifacius, His name is Rick Weible, 30 years computer expert, he said, Let me have a look at these. Within a few moments, he breached the iPad. Apple only fixed the way that he breached that iPad a few weeks ago. Think about that.

Hennepin County is currently trying to prevent me from getting the proof of that event. I may have to file to get that information, but Rick Weible has shown me email showing that Hennepin County was heavily suggesting that he reconsider his city council's decision to decline the use of these e poll pads, in 2016 the only municipality in Hennepin County in 2016 in that rollout that declined them. He also didn't like the contract.

Fourth point under trust.

Joe is right. These are the 10th generation. Actually, Angie is right too. They're not Wi Fi connected. Okay, but how else can you connect to the internet? One way is through a cellular connection. That is how these particular devices are connected to the internet. And they're always connected to the internet during the time that they're turned on.

Another way to think about it, how would you get the voter file from the state, from the statewide voter registration system, into that iPad without the Internet? How would you do it?

The second point related to that during the day, there's the capability through that internet connection to sync up and down data. So it's not only the Bluetooth that's printing out the little voter oath that you take over to get your ballot. There's voter data being synced back and forth.

Fourth, I not sure, but I believe that even Angie, if she asked for that information, would have a hard time getting it from KNOWiNK, which is a third party provider based out of St Louis, which has a really interesting background. We don't have enough time go into that. My three minutes are almost up.

So there is a small legislative point related to the architecture of these, relating to the internet. If you look up (Minnesota Statutes) §201.225, Subdivision 2, Part 11, I think, and many others do too, that these, because of that internet connection, put us in violation if we were to use them with that statute. That's really troubling for me, that we have that conflict with the state statute.

Okay, so that's trust. Internet connection is a big, big deal for me, but also just the hidden aspect of data, moving back and forth. When I worked at Target, that was a that was what I worked on. We worked on, how do we move data through these different systems? It matters how you think about it and how you set it up. But as the public in elections, we don't get to see that. KNOWiNK is not showing us that. And I could give you another description of how that's being hidden from us as well another time.

So I said trust, cost, and impact.

Cost.

I think the questions took care of that. But in the back, I don't remember your name, but the apples to apples comparison is what we're looking for if we if we were just focused on cost: What's the all in cost of current system versus a precinct using the poll pads? And of course, there's the cross sharing or the cost sharing aspect. So I think it's interesting that the state is subsidizing them.

Just that alone is interesting. But not only that, these systems as a product, they're evolving. So you look at the history of KNOWiNK once again.

Right now, Hennepin County is trying to prevent me from having the details of a pilot, which I'm pretty sure they ran last year, which allows these devices to be connected to a ballot printer. On-demand ballot printing in your precinct.

So think about it. You have data that's flowing back and forth, and you have the ability to print ballots that is potentially coming down the line. I think, unless we put our foot down on this one from an impact standpoint.

Oh, and I forgot to mention, but it was mentioned before. These are basically disposable. They only last a few elections. You got to replace them. There's a cost. There's concerns about that, especially in 2025.

So trust, cost, impact.

I think this choice is really impactful, because out of all the list of things that you could do locally where you have a voice and a say, whether it's in the township or the city or at the county, this is definitely one you have a decision on I think that's why there's so much emphasis on it right now.

I wasn't thinking about this in 2018 but many, many people are thinking, What can I do now? As they've started to question the overall electronic system, the legal aspect, there's 500 pages of statutes. I've looked at those in quite detail, and then you have all the processes, kind of behind the scenes. So this is one aspect of that overall picture. But if you ask me, Would I rather have an electronic tabulator, the scanners, or a poll pad? I'd rather not have both, but I might actually choose the tabulator.

By the way, the legislature as of 2023 says you don't have a choice if you use the tabulator before. Now you're stuck with them, but you still have a choice with the electronic pull pad.

So I've I strongly prefer paper for the reasons I mentioned, no internet connection, more secure. You understand how to use it. If it's a matter of training, you can increase the level of training and attention to detail to make sure everyone knows how to use it to reduce errors. And you kind of know what you're getting. And I'm just really in favor of that. From that perspective. There's a few other comments that I can make, but I think trust and cost are the two areas that I hear. And Derek has a comment.

DEREK: Yeah, my name is Derek Leon with ace that we were working on for three years.

The politics is changing on the poll pads in Anoka County. In 2018 we put them in all 21 cities. The things got old. It was time to renew them. We just had that debate. They had the exact same presentation in Anoka County. That's why we think it's coming from a second source.

ANGIE: No, I just created this, like, a couple hours ago.

DEREK: Well, it was very, very similar. I mean, different dollar amounts, but no criticism. Great presentation, but it was very similar, same talking points. What's important here is this time around, it went from a seven-zero vote back in 2018, two commissioners voted against the poll. Plus one commissioner—there are seven commissioners there—one Commissioner skipped that vote, so we ended up losing. But you can see the ball shifting up there. Their phones got lit up that people were telling them don't renew these poll pads. So I just wanted to have that. Thanks, Erik.

ERIK: Are there any brief questions? Otherwise, that's about all I have.

TODD: No. I would just want to say is, if anybody wants any more information, are you, you guys, able anybody reach out? Or is there a site to go to or anything?

DEREK: Yeah, we have website now (aceit.vote).

TODD: You do okay?

ANGIE: Yeah, you can reach out to me too, if you like.

TODD: One for both sides.

ERIK: If you approach me afterwards, I'm happy to give anyone my contact information directly.

QUESTION: There must be some pretty sophisticated encryption, Bluetooth data you talk about this floating around these devices. They're encrypted, aren't they, the data?

ERIK: So you talk about a Bluetooth. The Bluetooth is the Bluetooth allows this to print the receipt they take to the ballot judge. But then there's also built into this model, but a cellular he's talking about the data itself, between the between iPad that we have two or three iPads in there.

QUESTION: There's got to be some really sophisticated encryption going on so nobody can walk in with their own iPad and enter stuff data, right?

ERIK: Well, Joe, you want to comment on that? I have a couple of comments.

JOE: A comment because I actually, for numerous years, I've been an election judge. I have used these because in my precinct where I work, that's what they have.

The generation that they're buying, no county has the same problem, there's a 2018, they're buying new ones.

These are actually slightly different than the ones we've all used, because previous ones all had to connect to a hot spot and then cellular out. But that's also how they connected within the precinct. So this Bluetooth connection between the iPads, this will be the first time that they've been used in Anoka, sounds like it will be your guys' first time.

So we don't know about—we'll have to learn about it in our next judge training and everything—but this will be the first time they're being rolled out in regards to that.

And I want to the question in the back here, and I know we're having a lot of arguments with the state here, You do have a right to say, No.

County Commissioners could buy these, the auditor could say, We are going to use them, but under Minnesota statutes, they have to enter into an agreement with you. You have the right to say No.

#

I don't know what will happen in Isanti County, but I had a good feeling leaving the meeting that many in the room, apart from the staff, were on our side. If it came to a commissioner vote in Isant in the coming weeks, we thought, in talking with Derek, we might have the first instance of a commissioner group voting not to accept the iPads from KNOWiNK, and stay with paper.

Before concluding this short book, I want to turn briefly to a topic I raised in my short response to Angie, which described the evolving nature of the electronic poll pads, which, if attached to a ballot printer, also from KNOWiNK, can print on-demand ballots. This, again, was not a hypothetical, but a pilot program already conducted, according to documents and emails from Hennepin County, in 2024.

#

CHAPTER 7 - Hennepin County's Ballot Printer Pilot

#

Early 2025 had me digging into the contracts for Hennepin County with KNOWiNK so as to compare them with those already acquired in Anoka County. From there, through the data requests, I discovered there were amendments to the original contract, which alerted me to one of KNOWiNK's more recent products...

On-demand ballot printing could be coming down the pipeline and if the VOTER Accounts remain topped up, there is a bucket of money to be drawn from to fund them. The capability to have precinct level data, in a centralized way, and then print ballots on demand, is a powerful combination.

The uses for such a combination are several, which for the moment will leave to the reader's imagination. Let's take a look at Attachment 1B to Hennepin County's original A164895 KNOWiNK contract.

#

Attachment 1B

KNOWiNK, LLC.
460 N Lindbergh Blvd
Saint Louis, MO 63141
+1 8557655723
http://knowink.com

KNOWiNK

ADDRESS
Nicole Conlin
Hennepin County MN Board of
Elections
PO Box 1388
Minneapolis, MN 55440 USA

SHIP TO
Nicole Conlin
Hennepin County MN Board of
Elections
PO Box 1388
Minneapolis, MN 55440 USA

ESTIMATE #	DATE
6869	05/25/2023

DATE	ITEM	HARDWARE/SOFTWARE	QTY	UNIT PRICE	TOTAL AMOUNT
	Poll Print Connection Package	Includes: Redpark Ethernet Adapter Mikrotek Router Ethernet cables 9' lightning cable	5	250.00	1,250.00
	Curbside Case - Green		5	45.00	225.00
	Poll Print Printer		5	950.00	4,750.00
	Poll Print Cabinet - Blue		5	1,500.00	7,500.00
	Toner	Kyocera	5	150.00	750.00
	Poll Print Initial License	Includes First Year License for software updates and support.	5	1,000.00	5,000.00
	Setup and Training		1	2,500.00	2,500.00
	Poll Print Shipping		5	200.00	1,000.00
					Subtotal: 22,975.00
	Poll Print Annual License	Year 2 Includes software updates and support	5	500.00	2,500.00
	Poll Print Annual License	Year 3 Includes software updates and support	5	500.00	2,500.00
			TOTAL		USD 27,975.00

\#

Seeing this contract amendment then had me curious to know, What became of this 2024 pilot?

This email exchange between myself and Hennepin County shows that this pilot was indeed conducted. Notice the claim is that it wasn't 'completed' although it seems to fall short of acknowledging they started it. Why dance around this so much? Then the next line: "We are still evaluating the need..." I wonder what the need could possibly be.

Erik,

Hennepin County Elections did not complete this pilot in 2024 and would have no responsive data regarding it's results. We are still evaluating the need for this equipment as part of our operations in the future. We don't have plans to implement its use at this time.

If you have other requests for data related to this pilot, please direct those to the Hennepin County data request portal. Data Request Portal[1]

From: Erik <erikvanmechelen@proton.me>

Sent: Sunday, April 6, 2025 10:04 PM

To: Susan Fritze <Susan.Fritze@hennepin.us>

Subject: [External] Poll pad print roll out

#

Hi Susan,

What can you share about the results of the Hennepin County poll pad print pilot conducted in 2024? Is the pilot expected to continue or expand in 2025?

Thanks,

Erik

Disclaimer: If you are not the intended recipient of this message, please immediately notify the sender of the transmission error and then promptly permanently delete this message from your computer system.

#

---

1.   https://hennepincountymn.govqa.us/WEBAPP/_rs/supporthome.aspx

In case the reader is doubting whether Attachment 1B above is conclusive, let's take a look at Amendment 2 to Contract No: A164895, which I reproduce only in part below:

#

Contract No: **A164895** Amendment: **2**
AMENDMENT NO. 2 TO AGREEMENT NO. A164895

This Amendment No. 2 to Agreement No. A164895 is between the COUNTY OF HENNEPIN, STATE OF MINNESOTA, A-2300 Government Center, Minneapolis, Minnesota 55487, on behalf of the Hennepin County Elections ("COUNTY"), and Knowink LLC, 315 Lemay Ferry Road Suite 120, St. Louis, Missouri 63125 ("CONTRACTOR").

WHEREAS, under the Agreement, COUNTY purchased electronic poll book tablets and related hardware ("Purchased Hardware"), software, and services from CONTRACTOR;

WHEREAS, COUNTY wants to conduct a one-year pilot of CONTRACTOR's new poll printers;

The parties agree that Agreement No. A164895, including prior amendments if any, is amended as follows:

1. Section 2, SOFTWARE, HARDWARE, SERVICES, AND INTELLECTUAL PROPERTY, shall be amended to add the following to section 2(A) Software:

"Effective January 1, 2024, "Pilot Software" shall mean all software, applications, utilities and other related code, regardless of whether the aforementioned resides on COUNTY's computers, CONTRACTOR's computers, or other hosted computers, along with all updates that are made available to CONTRACTOR's other similarly situated customers, as further specified in Attachment 1B attached hereto.

As applicable throughout the Agreement, which shall be evidenced by usage and intent, the term "Software" shall include "Pilot Software"." Accordingly, the parties also expressly agree that CONTRACTOR's obligation to perform Services (as defined and specified in the Agreement, as amended) shall hereafter include performing Services for Pilot Software (referred to as "support" in Attachment 1B).

Commencing January 1, 2024 and continuing through December 31, 2024, CONTRACTOR grants to COUNTY a license: (i) to download, install, access, and use the Software in connection with COUNTY's business; and (ii) to download, install, access, use, modify, and configure a reasonable number of copies of the Software and/or documentation for redundancy, archival, testing, disaster recovery, and other purposes (may be referred to as the "Pilot Software License"). The Pilot Software License authorizes use by any five (5) concurrent COUNTY employees, contractors, or personnel.

Upon conclusion of the Pilot Software License, COUNTY may, in its sole discretion, elect to extend the Pilot Software License for an additional year. In no event shall a Pilot Software License renew/extend beyond expiration of the term of the Agreement.

Page **1** of **5**

Contract No: **A164895** Amendment: **2**

Notwithstanding similar provisions in Section 5 of the Agreement, the Pilot Software shall be covered by CONTRACTOR's standard (12) twelve month warranty ."

1. Section 2, SOFTWARE, HARDWARE, SERVICES, AND INTELLECTUAL PROPERTY, shall be amended to add the following to section 2(B) Hardware:

   "Effective January 1, 2024, "Pilot Hardware" shall mean poll print printers and related Hardware as further specified in Attachment 1B attached hereto, and including:

   1. - 5 Poll Print Printer
   2. - 5 Poll Print Connection Package
   3. - 5 Curbside Case – Green
   4. - 5 Poll Print Cabinet – Blue

5.   - 5 Toner

6.   As applicable throughout the Agreement, which shall be evidenced by usage and intent, the term "Hardware" shall include "Pilot Hardware". Accordingly, the parties also expressly agree that CONTRACTOR's obligation to perform Services (as defined and specified in the Agreement, as amended) shall hereafter include performing Services for Pilot Hardware (referred to as "support" in Attachment 1B).

   #

7.   The indicated quantities of Pilot Hardware may be adjusted upon subsequent written agreement of the parties. CONTRACTOR shall provide and transfer all right, title and interest in and to the Pilot Hardware as set forth herein. For clarification and not limitation, the parties acknowledge and agree that upon COUNTY's acceptance of any Pilot Hardware, including any Poll Print Printer(s) (or other Hardware), COUNTY shall own all right, title and interest in and to said Pilot Hardware, regardless of the expiration or termination of this Agreement or the Pilot Software license herein."

   #

But I was more interested in how this pilot went, what the need was, what the goals were, so I opened several data requests to try to learn more, including one asking for emails between MN OSS, Hennepin County, and KNOWiNK.

This is where it started to get interesting and I could sense I was onto something. One could imagine the back-and-forths between the administrator receiving the requests and then requesting the same from the various parties. It brings me small pleasure to know that the groups emails that were requested very likely know they are being audited, by me, and by I expect soon, many others all around Minnesota.

#

Hello Erik,

In regards to your email about your data request:

Email communications between MN OSS, Hennepin County, and KNOWiNK relating to "Pilot Software" and "Pilot Software License"referenced in Attachment 1B of AMENDMENT NO. 2 TO AGREEMENT NO. A164895, including these keywords:

- Pilot Software
- Pilot Software License
- Pilot Hardware
- Poll Print Printer
- Poll Print Printer Connection Package
- Poll Print Cabinet

#

There was limited communication between the three groups requested in the same communication and those that were included Hennepin County Attorneys which is confidential under attorney client privileges. -Chris

Chris Chiu | he/him/his
Hennepin County Elections
Chris.Chiu@hennepin.us | www.hennepin.us/elections[2]

#

Here we see confirmation of "limited communication between the three groups" and the excuse of attorney client privileges. It is my

2.　　　https://www.hennepin.us/elections

understanding that this is an erroneous response at that any contractual discussions must be shared. At some point I may have to file to release that information because it looks like it is being hidden from the public.

When I asked why I was getting this excuse, Mr. Chiu's response was to send an additional request on same. Here's that:

#

Hello Erik,

You may open another request through our data request portal.

No responsive data was found in the initial request :

Email communications between MN OSS, Hennepin County, and KNOWiNK relating to "Pilot Software" and "Pilot Software License"referenced in Attachment 1B of AMENDMENT NO. 2 TO AGREEMENT NO. A164895, including these keywords:

- Pilot Software
- Pilot Software License
- Pilot Hardware
- Poll Print Printer
- Poll Print Printer Connection Package
- Poll Print Cabinet

I am currently working on the other two that you have regarding training materials and communications for St. Boni. We had a massive influx of request following the 2024 election cycle.

-Chris

Chris Chiu | he/him/his

Hennepin County Elections

Chris.Chiu@hennepin.us | www.hennepin.us/elections[3]

From: Erik <erikvanmechelen@proton.me>

Sent: Monday, April 7, 2025 12:08 AM

To: Chris Chiu <Chris.Chiu@hennepin.us>

Subject: RE: [External] No responsive data - # D050203-010625

---

3.   https://www.hennepin.us/elections

Hi Chris,

Following up on this—I think that discussions of a contract are public information.

I'd like to re-open this request. Can you confirm?

Thanks,

Erik

On Friday, February 7th, 2025 at 1:20 PM, Erik <erikvanmechelen@proton.me> wrote:

Hi Chris,

Helpful reply, thank you!

It is indeed interesting that the preparation of deals/agreements for design/implementation of software/hardware which affects public outcomes directly can be hidden behind such reasons.

Again, though, thank you for including this detail for my knowledge and notes.

Thanks,

Erik

On Friday, February 7th, 2025 at 10:00 AM, Chris Chiu <Chris.Chiu@hennepin.us> wrote:

#

Hello Erik,

In regards to your email about your data request:

Email communications between MN OSS, Hennepin County, and KNOWiNK relating to "Pilot Software" and "Pilot Software License" referenced in Attachment 1B of AMENDMENT NO. 2 TO AGREEMENT NO. A164895, including these keywords:

- Pilot Software
- Pilot Software License
- Pilot Hardware
- Poll Print Printer
- Poll Print Printer Connection Package

- Poll Print Cabinet

#

There was limited communication between the three groups requested in the same communication and those that were included Hennepin County Attorneys which is confidential under attorney client privileges. -Chris

Chris Chiu | he/him/his
Hennepin County Elections
Chris.Chiu@hennepin.us | www.hennepin.us/elections[4]
From: Erik <erikvanmechelen@proton.me>
Sent: Monday, February 3, 2025 5:22 PM
To: Ambur L Klein <Ambur.Klein@hennepin.us>
Cc: Chris Chiu <Chris.Chiu@hennepin.us>
Subject: [External] No responsive data - # D050203-010625

#

Ambur, Chris,

Able to provide any context? Seems odd that county would have adopted agreement for new tech without any communication with the vendor they are purchasing from.

If can guide me to a better prompt, please do. I am quite a patient and persistent person.

Thanks,

Erik

#

Disclaimer: If you are not the intended recipient of this message, please immediately notify the sender of the transmission error and then promptly permanently delete this message from your computer system.

---

4.   https://www.hennepin.us/elections

Disclaimer: If you are not the intended recipient of this message, please immediately notify the sender of the transmission error and then promptly permanently delete this message from your computer system.

#

The lesson for anyone trying to get government information, which Chapter 13 of Minnesota Statutes governs—it's all public unless classified—is to know how to ask and to be persistent. There are cases from around the country as well as locally where suits have been filed to force the release of data which should have been given over without any delay.

It is a fear of some that the evasiveness to the discovery of the pilot that Hennepin County obviously ran in 2024, as shown in Amendment 2 above, suggests that this is far from the end of the electronic poll pad story and their potential capability.

Just imagine, for a moment, the ability to print on-demand ballots at the precinct level while simultaneously having access to real-time precinct voter data in a centralized way. One of my favorite mathmeticians, Draza Smith, has commented recently that elections are a precinct game. In-house ballot printers would make elections quite the game indeed. Nothing in Minnesota statutes seems to have prevented such a pilot from being run, but since the pilot was apparently 'not completed', whatever that means, the public has been blocked, so far, from learning anything more about this.

The reader may also like to note that Hennepin County Elections Manager Ginny Gelms, party to the initial pressure that St. Bonifacius came under in 2016, and still the Elections Manager today, in 2025, despite in 2024 not using party-balanced election judges for the absentee ballot boards for the first 40 of 45 days of absentee voting (about 200,000 ballots), has not responded to any of my emails regarding this pilot program. This is unsurprising, as nor could she provide any absentee data I asked for during the Hennepin County Canvassing Board Meeting (the certification meeting) despite that being the venue where the five-member board would certify Hennepin's 2024 election. In that meeting, I was told I couldn't speak, but politely asked again, about the absentee numbers, which were not shared.

#

NEXT STEPS FOR MINNESOTA

#

In this review of the status of *one* of Minnesota's precinct-level election sensors, also known as electronic poll pads, we've covered:

- Mayor Rick Weible's St. Bonifacius decision not to use the KNOWiNK poll pads in 2016 after hacking into the demo product as well as noting serious problems with the proposed contract from Hennepin County; he was able to withstand pressure from Hennepin County to use them despite these concerns

- The 2013 Electronic Roster Task Force's Findings and Recommendations which paved the way for legislation, including Minnesota Statutes §201.225, a pivotal statute that the people, cities, counties, and the state are currently in debate about

- Mayor of Oak Grove (Anoka County) Weston Rolf's leadership in canceling the poll pad agreement in 2024, and again in 2025, and Ramsey's (also Anoka County) decision to do so as well

- The felony threat from the Anoka County Elections Department letter in late October 2024, presumably signed off on by County Attorney Brad Johnson, a letter which also quoted Secretary of State Steve Simon

- The 4-2 vote on replacement iPads in early 2025 for Anoka County's 128 precincts, which saw not one (1) but two (2) commissioners raise concerns; John Heinrich noted the potential for scalable fraud, while Jeff Reinert promoted city autonomy and suggested the wisdom of asking cities if they wanted them before purchasing

- Isanti County's upcoming decision after considering a thorough presentation from County Auditor Angie Larson and a brief response from a researcher and historian from South Minneapolis which took place on April 24, 2025 in the Isanti County Government Center

#

Of all the things that local decision makers, such as city councilmembers, town board supervisors, and county commissioners, could do to promote transparency in local elections, removing electronic poll pads, or refusing to buy them, and using paper poll books instead—including improving that process—is probably the most significant and impactful decision to implement right Now in April and May of 2025.

At minimum, those using paper will know that the data stored on that paper is likely not leaving the precinct. At best, those areas will not be actively using sensors which allow a centralized system to engineer results electronically in sophisticated ways.

#

AUTHOR'S NOTE (VERSION 1, APRIL 30, 2025)

#

As with any documentation that happens close to the event, there can be missed opportunities because the greater context was complex or because I simply didn't see or understand something yet.

Because time is of the essence—the electronic poll pad rollouts continue as you read—providing decision makers with a balanced and informed view of this lesser-known aspect of the election process is key, but one cannot get all the details down on such a subject, especially when our own government withholds key information, as demonstrated in the chapter about the Hennepin County on-demand ballot printing pilot.

Documents will periodically be added to https://projectminnesota.com/documents that are relevant to understanding or further researching claims made in this book. For instance, much can be gleaned from the 2013 Electronic Roster Task Force: Findings & Recommendations from the Office of the Secretary of State, published on January 31, 2014, or by carefully reading the back and forth between myself and the Hennepin County staff assigned to respond to data requests.

For any that are early to read this, feedback is definitely welcome, as I am able to update the book in later versions, as I have done with *[S]elections in Minnesota*, now in 2025 in its third version after its original publicaiton in June 2022. Meanwhile, for those interested in my political background—I think almost anyone living in Minneapolis or the Greater Twin Cities has become political based simply upon current events—I invite you to read *Auditing Minnesota: The 2022 SOS Campaign*, which talks about how I learned that political parties control the candidates, and computers control the results.

#

—Erik van Mechelen, April 30, 2025

#

FURTHER READING

#

[S]elections in Minnesota: An Introduction to How Machines Controlled 2020

   Auditing Minnesota: The 2022 SOS Campaign

\#

Both books available as Ebook or Paperback
    Buy online or request from your local bookstore

\#

HAVE A STORY TO TELL?

\#

Contact   the   author   to   arrange   a   phone   call:
erikvanmechelen@proton.me

Don't miss out!

Visit the website below and you can sign up to receive emails whenever Erik van Mechelen publishes a new book. There's no charge and no obligation.

https://books2read.com/r/B-A-FVZIB-VIYGG

BOOKS 2 READ

Connecting independent readers to independent writers.

Also by Erik van Mechelen

AUDITING MN
Auditing Minnesota: The 2022 SOS Campaign
Simon's Sensors: The Secret of the iPads

Standalone
Selections in Minnesota: Consequences of the 2020 Election and How
to Reclaim Control of Our Government

Watch for more at https://projectminnesota.com.

9 798230 973737